WOMEN'S PRO BASKETBALL TODAY

CREATIVE EDUCATION

THE HISTORY OF THE LOS ANGELES

SPARKS

JULIE L. NELSON

Published by Creative Education
123 South Broad Street, Mankato, Minnesota 56001
Creative Education is an imprint of The Creative Company

Design by Stephanie Blumenthal
Cover design by Kathy Petelinsek
Production design by Andy Rustad

Photos by: NBA Photos

Library of Congress Cataloging-in-Publication Data

Nelson, Julie L.
The History of the Los Angeles Sparks / by Julie L. Nelson
p. cm. — (Women's Pro Basketball Today)
Summary: describes the history of the Los Angeles Sparks professional women's
basketball team and profiles some of their leading players.
ISBN 1-58341-014-7

1. Los Angeles Sparks (Basketball team) Juvenile literature. 2. Basketball for women—United States
Juvenile literature. [1. Los Angeles Sparks (Basketball team) 2. Women basketball players
3. Basketball players.] I. Title. II. Series.

GV885.52.L68N45 1999
796.323'64'0979494—dc21   99-18890
                                                                                                                            CIP

First Edition

2 4 6 8 9 7 5 3 1

On June 21, 1997, Penny Toler of the Los Angeles Sparks scored the first points in the history of the Women's National Basketball Association, ushering in a new era of women's basketball—an era of unprecedented fan excitement and national television exposure. But most importantly to the players, the league opened new doors of opportunity in the U.S. for the finest female athletes in the world. "You'll see a level above what you're used to seeing at the college level," promised Sparks standout Lisa Leslie. "We're more aggressive, stronger, and faster." Running the same floor as famous Los Angeles Lakers teams of the past, Leslie and the Sparks promise to maintain a high level of summer basketball in California for years to come.

PENNY TOLER NETTED

THE WNBA'S FIRST

FIELD GOAL.

A LEAGUE OF THEIR OWN

Before the WNBA was born, there had been numerous unsuccessful attempts to launch professional women's basketball leagues in the United States. The most recent, the American Basketball League (ABL), debuted in October 1996 and folded in December 1998. In 1992, the Women's World Basketball Association attempted to establish a six-team league in the Midwest which quickly fizzled. Another league, the Women's Professional Basketball League, debuted in 1978 with eight teams and survived only three seasons.

It was clear from the start, however, that the WNBA was going to be different. The successful and lucrative National Basketball Association supported the creation of the league, and an aggressive advertising campaign was launched with television and print ads echoing the league slogan, "We got next." Teams would be located only in cities with NBA franchises and arenas in which to play, and the WNBA season would be held between the months of June and August—a schedule that kept the leagues from competing for fans.

Rules for the WNBA would be nearly identical to those of the women's college game: two 20-minute halves, a 19-foot-9 three-point line, a 30-second shot clock, and 10-player rosters. The league's first president would be Val Ackerman, whose basketball

BACKUP POINT GUARD JAMILA WIDEMAN

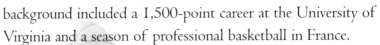

background included a 1,500-point career at the University of Virginia and a season of professional basketball in France.

After playing abroad, Ackerman went on to law school and later worked in various positions within the NBA. She continued to stay active with women's basketball, however, and helped to create the U.S. Women's National Team, a collection of the United States' most talented players, including Lisa Leslie, Rebecca Lobo, and Sheryl Swoopes. The team, which would eventually capture gold in the 1996 Olympics, played against college and international teams worldwide in 1995 and 1996, compiling a 60–0 record.

Three months after the Games in Atlanta, the WNBA announced the eight charter cities of the new league: Charlotte, Cleveland, Houston, New York, Phoenix, Sacramento, Salt Lake City, and Los Angeles. It was time to draft players and build rosters for the most heralded women's league of all time.

THE INAUGURAL SPARKS

Lisa Leslie, one of the most recognizable names in women's basketball in the 1990s, was one of the first three players signed to the WNBA. While many of her former Olympic team-mates chose to play in the rival ABL, Leslie took a chance with the WNBA and was assigned to the Los Angeles Sparks, the sister team to the NBA's Lakers.

As one of a handful of "franchise" players assigned to the league's first teams, the 6-foot-5 center was no

stranger to California basketball fans. After a successful career at Morningside High School in Inglewood, California, Leslie went on to rewrite the record books at the University of Southern California, setting new marks for blocked shots in a season and a career. She also set the Pac-10 Conference record for career points and rebounds and was named National Player of the Year as a senior. Before joining the WNBA, Leslie played one season of professional basketball in Italy and capped her 1996 Olympic experience with a masterful 29-point performance in the gold-medal game.

Like most professional female players returning to America after playing in foreign leagues, Leslie saw the WNBA as an exciting opportunity to showcase the athletic abilities of women. "I like that I can help to change people's perspectives about what women can and can't do," the center said. "And when my playing days are over, I hope people will remember me as the most versatile center to ever play the game—man or woman."

With the multitalented Leslie, the Sparks had arguably the league's best center around which to build their roster. The team's second addition would be Penny Toler, a 5-foot-8 guard equally skilled at scoring and distributing the ball. Toler, who had played college ball at Long Beach State before a successful eight-year professional career in Europe, also gave the Sparks some valuable veteran experience in the backcourt.

PAMELA MCGEE (ABOVE);

VERSATILE MWADI

MABIKA (BELOW)

FAN FAVORITE HAIXIA ZHENG

On February 27, 1997, the WNBA held its Elite Draft, which was intended to spread 16 talented veteran players around the league. With its picks, Los Angeles selected two post players: 6-foot-3 forward Daedra Charles and 6-foot-8 center Haixia Zheng. Although Charles would see limited playing time in her one season with the Sparks, Zheng would quickly become a fan favorite.

Zheng was born in the Henan Province of China, and her early career highlights included dominating performances for the Chinese National Team. In 1989, the big center scored a record 67 points against the Soviet National Team. In the 1996 Summer Games, Zheng averaged 18.1 points and nine rebounds per contest. Sparks management saw Zheng's incredible size and strength as the perfect complement to Leslie's finesse game.

In a second WNBA draft held in April, the league's eight teams took turns choosing from other unsigned veterans and the newest class of graduating college seniors. With their picks, the Sparks selected a trio of guards: Jamila Wideman, Tamecka Dixon, and Katrina Colleton.

As a high school senior, Wideman's state championship team in Massachusetts had been chronicled in the best-selling book, *In These Girls, Hope is a Muscle.* The 5-foot-6 Wideman went on to an unprecedented Stanford career as a four-year captain and starter, leading her team to three consecutive Final Four appearances.

Soon after the 21-year-old was featured on the cover of

Sports Illustrated on March 17, 1997, the Sparks took the multitalented guard with their first pick in the draft. Wideman knew that the

FIRST ROUND PICK JAMILA WIDEMAN (ABOVE); DEFENSIVE FORCE KATRINA COLLETON (LEFT)

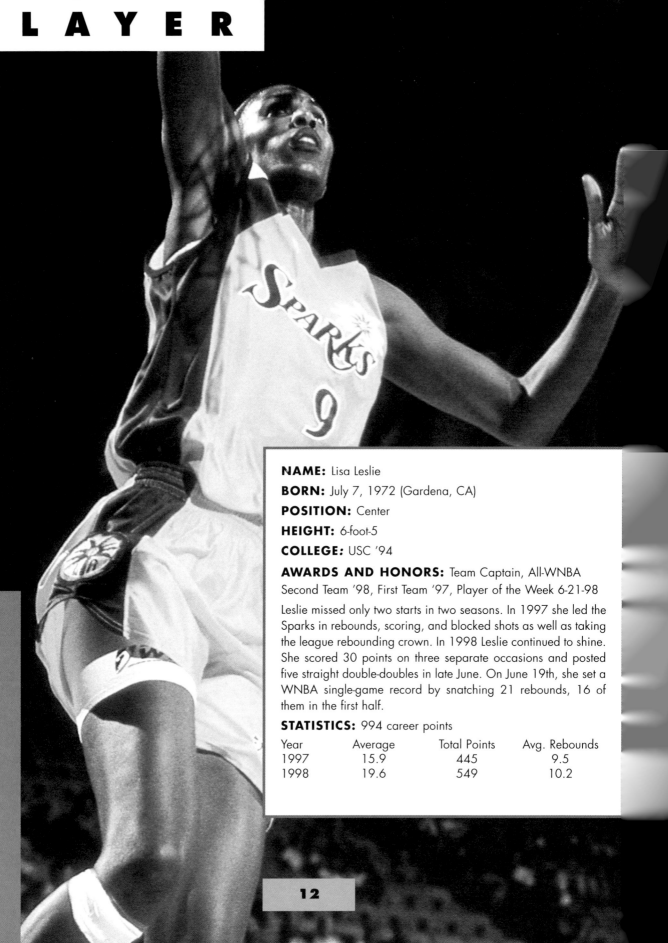

NAME: Lisa Leslie

BORN: July 7, 1972 (Gardena, CA)

POSITION: Center

HEIGHT: 6-foot-5

COLLEGE: USC '94

AWARDS AND HONORS: Team Captain, All-WNBA Second Team '98, First Team '97, Player of the Week 6-21-98

Leslie missed only two starts in two seasons. In 1997 she led the Sparks in rebounds, scoring, and blocked shots as well as taking the league rebounding crown. In 1998 Leslie continued to shine. She scored 30 points on three separate occasions and posted five straight double-doubles in late June. On June 19th, she set a WNBA single-game record by snatching 21 rebounds, 16 of them in the first half.

STATISTICS: 994 career points

Year	Average	Total Points	Avg. Rebounds
1997	15.9	445	9.5
1998	19.6	549	10.2

NAME: Tamecka Dixon

BORN: December 14, 1975 (Linden, N.J.)

POSITION: Guard

HEIGHT: 5-foot-9

COLLEGE: Kansas '97

AWARDS AND HONORS: WNBA Player of the Week 8-10-97

A second-round draft pick, Dixon led her teammates in three-pointers and steals in 1997, and was second in the WNBA for three-point percentage. In 1998 she continued to improve, ranking among the league's top 10 overall scorers. She tallied a career-best 26 points in a game against Detroit but missed the last eight games of the season due to a knee injury.

STATISTICS: 677 career points

Year	Average	Total Points	Avg. Assists
1997	11.9	320	2.0
1998	16.2	357	2.5

PORTRAIT

13

groundbreaking league was a unique opportunity. "We know what it's like not to have professional role models," she said, referring to the previous lack of women's leagues, "and our challenge is to make sure the young players in the game see that there are role models."

With their next pick, the Sparks took sharp-shooting guard Tamecka Dixon, who had just capped her college career at Kansas with Big 12 Player of the Year honors. Los Angeles then completed its balanced guard lineup by drafting Katrina Colleton, a 5-foot-10 defensive specialist with a year of professional experience in Israel.

A month before the season began, the Sparks rounded out their roster by signing Linda Burgess, a 6-foot-1 forward, and Mwadi Mabika, a 20-year-old guard and the league's youngest player. Despite her youth, Mabika had played seven professional seasons in Greece and her homeland of Zaire (now the Congo) before joining the WNBA.

With their roster filled out and under the direction of head coach Linda Sharp, the Sparks couldn't wait to begin their first WNBA season. After a short preseason camp, it was time to play ball.

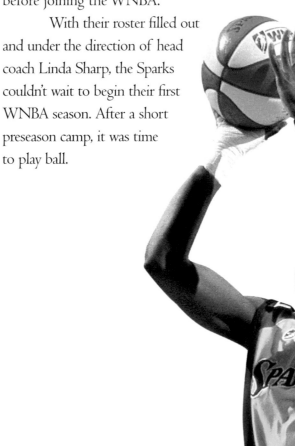

SANDRA VANEMBRICQS

TIMICHA KIRBY

(ABOVE); HAIXIA

ZHENG (BELOW)

DOWN TO THE WIRE

The Sparks' first season in the WNBA began with a nationally televised home game against the New York Liberty. More than 14,000 fans witnessed the historic occasion as Lisa Leslie led her team onto the floor to face Rebecca Lobo, Teresa Weatherspoon, and the Liberty. League president Val Ackerman tossed the ball up at midcourt for the ceremonial tip-off, and the WNBA was underway.

Unfortunately, the Sparks would have to wait another day for their first win, as the Liberty broke an early tie and led the rest of the way, winning 67–57. Regardless of the outcome, however, players from both teams found the game exhilarating. "It felt great to finally be out there playing ball," Rebecca Lobo summed up. "We don't have to worry about 'We have two days left, we've got next.' We're here now."

After losing again at Utah, Los Angeles welcomed the Charlotte Sting to the Great Western Forum and notched its first victory of the season, 74–54. Tamecka Dixon, who had struggled offensively in the first two games, scored 16 points in the first half, including a buzzer-beater just before the break. "We're improving," said Leslie, who put up 19 points in the win. "We played for 40 minutes and played like we wanted it."

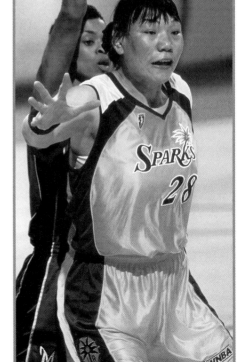

The towering Zheng would dominate the Sparks' next victory, a 93–73 drubbing of the Sacramento Monarchs. She collected 28 points, pulled down 10 rebounds, and made all eight of her free throws. "I'm just happy to win," she said. "My confidence is good. I was able to establish my position in the low post, and my teammates got me the ball when I had very good position."

Next came the Houston Comets—who would go on to claim the WNBA championship—and their star Cynthia Cooper. With 6.7 seconds left in an exciting back-and-forth game, Houston's Wanda Guyton scored to send the game into overtime, and the Comets pulled away to win 71–66. Although their team lost, Sparks fans were treated to an incredible 21-point, 16-rebound performance by Leslie.

The Sparks finally claimed their first win on the road on July 3 with a 74–62 victory in Cleveland. Two games later, Sparks forward Linda Burgess burned the Utah Starzz with 20 points in an impressive debut start. Although several Sparks' players had shown star potential in the team's first 10 games, a loss at Sacramento on July 15 dropped Los Angeles' record to a dismal 4–7. Sparks management decided it was time for a change.

PENNY TOLER AVERAGED 13 PPG IN '97 (ABOVE); SPARKS SHOW TEAM SPIRIT (BELOW).

Head coach Linda Sharp was fired and replaced by assistant coach Julie Rousseau, who responded by making two major changes: increasing Zheng's playing time and moving Tamecka Dixon from small forward to her normal guard position. Zheng responded immediately by posting 15 points in a 77–52 win over the Comets. "They were working their zone very well, and inside they were too big for us," Houston coach Van Chancellor said of the resurgent Sparks. "If L.A. continues to play like that, they will be the team to beat."

The Sparks next traveled to New York's Madison Square Garden, where the 11–1 New York Liberty had amassed a 6–0 home record. An energetic crowd of 16,236 fans looked on as the Sparks fell 69–57.

Los Angeles would suffer two more losses before halting its losing streak with an overtime win against Phoenix. Dixon scored three critical points in the final 18 seconds of overtime to put the Sparks ahead for good in only their second road win of the year. Leslie again led the Sparks in scoring with 17. "Even though we had lost the last two, we have been playing much better," she pointed out. "A team with this much talent took a lot longer to get our chemistry together. We played with a lot of emotion tonight."

In the next contest, an 84–62 victory at Sacramento, the always-dangerous Dixon netted 20 points—16 of them in the second half—and added eight rebounds and four assists. The Sparks'

winning streak continued with a 91–69 rout of Utah, pulling Los Angeles within a game and a half of Western Conference-leading Phoenix with only a month remaining in the season.

A FURIOUS FINALE

The Sparks started the month of August with an 81–57 loss to Houston, as WNBA scoring leader Cynthia Cooper—who would soon be named the league's Most Valuable Player—racked up 34 points for the Comets.

The Sparks would split their next four games, including a satisfying win at New York before the league's second-largest crowd of 16,944. Tamecka Dixon continued her surprisingly strong play and was named WNBA Player of the Week after leading the Sparks in scoring three straight games. "Tamecka Dixon has been unbelievable ever since she figured it out that she's unstoppable," Coach Rousseau said.

By mid-August, the Sparks were 10–13 and trailing the Phoenix Mercury in the race for the WNBA's last playoff spot with only five games left. Facing long odds, Los Angeles rose to the challenge, sweeping four straight games—its longest winning streak of the season.

Leslie and Zheng combined for 39 points in the first victory, a 10-point win over Utah. Los Angeles then pulled within a game of Phoenix by beating the Mercury 75–66. Leslie again dominated with 26 points and 15 boards, while Dixon continued to cruise with 23 points. The Sparks' third straight win was more dramatic; with less than a second on the clock, Burgess hit two free throws to seal a 78–76 win over the playoff-bound Liberty.

ACQUIRED FROM

SACRAMENTO,

PAM MCGEE

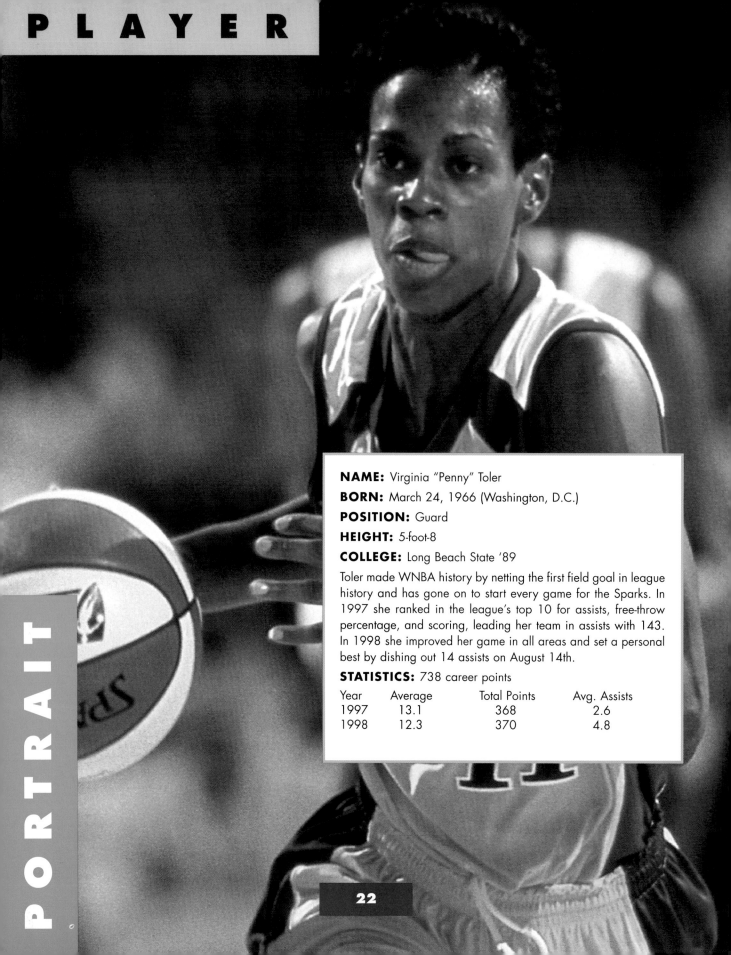

PORTRAIT

NAME: Virginia "Penny" Toler

BORN: March 24, 1966 (Washington, D.C.)

POSITION: Guard

HEIGHT: 5-foot-8

COLLEGE: Long Beach State '89

Toler made WNBA history by netting the first field goal in league history and has gone on to start every game for the Sparks. In 1997 she ranked in the league's top 10 for assists, free-throw percentage, and scoring, leading her team in assists with 143. In 1998 she improved her game in all areas and set a personal best by dishing out 14 assists on August 14th.

STATISTICS: 738 career points

Year	Average	Total Points	Avg. Assists
1997	13.1	368	2.6
1998	12.3	370	4.8

NAME: Orlando Woolridge

BORN: December 16, 1959

POSITION: Head Coach

SEASONS COACHED: 1998–present

RECORD: 5-5

On July 31, 1998, Orlando Woolridge become the first former NBA player to take on head coaching responsibilities with the WNBA. Woolridge was taken as the sixth overall choice in the 1981 NBA Draft and played 13 seasons with Chicago, Los Angeles, and Philadelphia before finishing his professional career in Italy. Woolridge began his career with the Sparks as a talent scout, and in June of 1997 he was elevated to assistant coach. In the midst of a disappointing second season, he was promoted to head coach. The Sparks responded well to their new coach, winning their first three games, finishing 5-5 under Woolridge.

PORTRAIT

Two nights later, the Sparks treated their home crowd to an 88–77 win over Sacramento. Zheng and Toler made sure the team's final 1997 home game was a memorable one by posting 21 and 19 points, respectively. Team leader Lisa Leslie credited such balanced team play for the Sparks' late surge. "I'm not surprised we turned it around this year," she said. "I see the team chemistry that we have, and we are developing more and more as we play together on the floor."

On August 24, the Sparks traveled to Phoenix, trailing the Mercury by just one game in the Western Conference. After 40 hard-fought minutes, the score was knotted up at 64–64. Things looked bleak for the Sparks early in the extra session, as the

Mercury scored the first seven points. Penny Toler then answered with four points to cut the lead to 71–68 with under a minute to play. The Sparks' desperation three-pointer in the waning moments, however, missed the mark, ending Los Angeles' season.

Despite the team's bitter loss, many Sparks' players finished their first WNBA season with impressive numbers. Lisa Leslie, who was named to the All-WNBA First Team, led the league with 9.5 rebounds per game and was third in scoring with a 15.9 average. Haixia Zheng, recipient of the 1997 WNBA Sportsmanship Award, led the league with a .618 scoring percentage from the field. The versatile Penny Toler finished among the top 10 in the league in scoring and assists, and Tamecka Dixon overcame a slow start to become one of the league's premiere shooting guards, scoring 25 in the season's final game.

A NEW SEASON

Before the 1998 season, the Sparks added some young blood to the roster by drafting two 22-year-olds: guard Allison Feaster, a standout at Harvard, and Octavia Blue, a 6-foot-1 forward. Center Eugenia Rycraw and forward Sandra VanEmbricqs, both veterans with overseas experience, were also assigned to the Sparks. On April 6, the Sparks traded forward Linda Burgess to the Sacramento Monarchs for center Pam McGee, who had posted a respectable 10.6 points per game in 1997.

The Sparks' second season would be a disappointing one plagued by injuries and a lack of team chemistry, but

GUARD ALLISON

FEASTER (ABOVE);

YOUNG FORWARD

OCTAVIA BLUE (BELOW)

their debut at Utah showed no sign of the problems to come. The Sparks won 89–83 on strong play from Leslie (24 points and 12 rebounds), who had just rejoined the team two days earlier after playing in Germany in the offseason. "I don't know if we sent a message or not," Leslie said, "but I think it's going to be a good season for the Sparks."

The Sparks then suffered two straight defeats and lost talented rookie Allison Feaster for the season with a broken foot. On June 19, they rebounded with a solid win in their home-court debut against a powerful New York squad. Leslie set a WNBA record with 21 boards in the 78–75 win, while Haixia Zheng added 19 points, and the always-reliable Tamecka Dixon added 15.

A rough patch would then follow, as the Sparks dropped five straight games and lost Zheng for the season to injury. L.A. finally snapped the streak on July 7 with an 86–79 win over Charlotte, high-scorers Leslie and Dixon combined for 43 points.

The Sparks reached the mid-season point with a mere 5–9 record and would continue to struggle, dropping games to Houston, New York, Cleveland, and the expansion Detroit Shock. Leslie, the team's scoring leader, missed two games with a knee injury, and by July 29, the Sparks were 6–13 and dwelling near the basement of the Western Conference.

ERIN ALEXANDER (ABOVE);

INJURY KEPT ALLISON

FEASTER OUT OF THE

LINEUP (RIGHT).

Once again, it was time for Sparks management to make a change. Coach Rousseau was fired, and assistant coach Orlando Woolridge was promoted in her place. Woolridge was no stranger to basketball success nor the L.A. basketball scene. The Sparks' third head coach in less than two years had played for the dominant Lakers from 1981 to 1994 and had earned a reputation as their most artistic dunker. Woolridge had finished his career playing in Italy before taking a job with the Sparks as a scout and then an assistant coach.

The change gave the Sparks a much-needed boost as they upset the visiting Phoenix Mercury decisively, 71–56. "This team is playing with a lot of confidence right now," Woolridge said after his team won again at Utah. "We're finding the way to maintain our composure."

The team's eighth win came at a cost, however, as guard Tamecka Dixon injured her left knee with less than two minutes remaining in the game. Unfortunately, Dixon's knee injury would sideline her for the remainder of the season, and the Sparks struggled in their remaining seven games, going 2–5, including an embarrassing loss to the 3–22 Mystics before a national television audience.

Leslie continued to lead the Sparks in scoring, pouring in 30 points twice in August, and Toler, McGee, and Mabika did their best to make up for the loss of Dixon and Zheng, averaging between 14.6 and 7.6 points per game during the final month. "Leslie and Toler played well, but that's what you expect from

VETERAN SANDRA

VANEMBRICQS (ABOVE);

FORMER LAKER ORLANDO

WOOLRIDGE (BELOW)

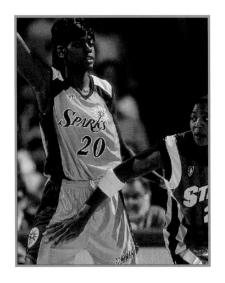

our team leaders," Woolridge said, crediting balanced teamwork for the Sparks' stronger play late in the season. "We're trying to build a foundation for next year."

The Sparks' final game of 1998 came on the road against the Houston Comets, who would soon repeat as WNBA champions. An 80–71 loss left Los Angeles in third place in the final Western Conference standings with a 12–18 record. Although the season again ended on a frustrating note, the Sparks went down with all guns blazing. Leslie led the Sparks' scoring attack once again with 24, while Toler racked up 19 and reserve forward Octavia Blue added 13.

THE FUTURE OF A TEAM AND LEAGUE

The Sparks have good reason for optimism in 1999. Penny Toler has established herself as a strong floor leader equally adept at scoring and creating plays for her teammates, and fellow guard Dixon can dominate games with her spectacular shooting.

To no one's surprise, Lisa Leslie has proven herself to be one of the premiere women's players in the world. In 1998, she finished among the top 20 leaders in eight statistical categories and was named to the All-WNBA Second Team. But most importantly, Leslie believes in the future of the team "I love the nucleus of this team," the center said. "That core has the potential to play the style of basketball that we want in L.A.—a fast-breaking, fast-paced,

SHARP SHOOTER TAMECKA DIXON

CENTER EUGENIA

RYCRAW (ABOVE);

TEAM CAPTAIN

LISA LESLIE (RIGHT)

high-intensity defensive style. I really believe we can have that here if we keep building."

Some of the tools in the building process still on the horizon include the 1999 class of college players, as well as potential crossovers from the dissolved American Basketball League. With the University of Tennessee standout Chamique Holdsclaw joining veterans such as Dawn Staley and Teresa Edwards on the WNBA court, the league's talent pool should be deeper than ever.

The WNBA expanded to 12 teams in 1999 with Minnesota and Orlando franchises entering the mix, and excitement around the league can only improve with the infiltration of ABL talent. The first two seasons were a smashing success in many regards: consistently competitive play, high merchandise sales, and strong fan support. With the league on the rise, Lisa Leslie and her Sparks teammates hope to rise to new heights as well and light a championship fire in Los Angeles.